OUT OF THIS WORLD

Meet NASA Inventor Geoffrey Landis and His Team's

Land-Sailing Venus Rover

WORLD
BOOK

www.worldbook.com

World Book, Inc.
180 North LaSalle Street
Suite 900
Chicago, Illinois 60601
USA

For information about other World Book publications, visit our website at www.worldbook.com or call 1-800-WORLDBK (967-5325).

For information about sales to schools and libraries, call 1-800-975-3250 (United States), or 1-800-837-5365 (Canada).

Library of Congress Cataloging-in-Publication Data for this volume has been applied for.

Out of This World
978-0-7166-6155-9 (set, hc.)

Land-Sailing Venus Rover
ISBN: 978-0-7166-6160-3 (hc.)

Also available as:
ISBN: 978-0-7166-6169-6 (e-book)

Printed in China by Shenzhen Donnelley Printing Co., Ltd., Guangdong Province
1st printing June 2017

Staff

Writer: Jeff De La Rosa

Contents

Glossary There is a glossary of terms on page 45. Terms defined in the glossary are in boldface type that **looks like this** on their first appearance on any spread (two facing pages).

Pronunciations (how to say words) are given in parentheses the first time some difficult words appear in the book. They look like this: pronunciation (pruh NUHN see AY shuhn).

Introduction

Look in the night sky just after sunset, or in the early morning sky just before sunrise, and you may see an extremely bright "star" close to the horizon. That "star" is actually the planet Venus. Like the other planets in our solar system, Venus shines with light reflected from the sun. But Venus appears brighter than the other planets in part because it is so close to Earth—closer than any other planet.

In cosmic terms, Venus is our next-door neighbor. So we might expect to know a lot about the planet's surface. After all, the planet Mars is nearly twice as far away, and we have sent dozens of **probes** there. Every year, **orbiters** send back breathtaking images of Martian landscapes. **Landers** and **rovers** have even dug in the Martian soil and drilled into Martian rock.

Next to the moon,
Venus is the brightest
object in the night sky.

Despite its closeness, the surface of Venus remains mostly a mystery. Why don't we know more about our closest neighbor? Studying the planet from orbit is difficult because it is covered in an unbroken layer of thick clouds. Orbiting **probes** require specialized equipment, such as radar, to peer through the haze. Potential **landers** are faced with even more problems. Those thick clouds are acidic and can damage spacecraft parts. Beneath the clouds, extremely high temperatures and pressures would melt and crush landers.

A handful of landers have actually been sent to the surface of Venus. But with the extreme conditions, even the most durable lander worked for only about two hours after landing. How can we study a planet that can so quickly destroy our equipment?

Scientist Geoffrey Landis wants to overcome all of that. Landis is working to design not just a lander, but a **rover** that could conduct an extended exploration of Venus's surface. Landis envisions a craft that could not only survive in the extreme conditions on the surface of Venus, but even make use of them. His craft would harness winds in the planet's thick atmosphere to "sail" around the Venusian surface.

The NASA Innovative Advanced Concepts program. The titles in the *Out of This World* series feature projects that have won grant money from a group formed by the United States National Aeronautics and Space Administration, or NASA. The NASA Innovative Advanced Concepts program (NIAC) provides funding to teams working to develop bold new advances in space technology. You can visit NIAC's website at www.nasa.gov/niac.

Meet Geoffrey Landis.

❚❚ Hello, I'm a science fiction writer and a scientist at NASA's John Glenn Research Center in Cleveland, Ohio. For years, I have worked on rover missions exploring the surface of Mars. Now I hope to harness the wind to explore a much more challenging environment—the surface of Venus. ❚❚

Destination: Venus

Venus is one of Earth's neighbors in the solar system. Venus is the second planet from the sun, and Earth is the third. No other planet comes nearer to Earth than does Venus. At its closest approach, Venus is "only" about 23.7 million miles (38.2 million kilometers) away.

Venus is nearly the exact same size as Earth. Both planets have a rocky surface and thick atmosphere. They have roughly the same mass (amount of matter) and similar gravitational pulls.

While Venus and Earth share many similarities, Venus is home to one of the most alien environments in our solar system. The atmosphere of Venus is heavier than that of any other planet. It consists primarily of **carbon dioxide.** Carbon dioxide makes up less than 1 percent of Earth's atmosphere. Venus's atmosphere is extremely dry, with only small amounts of water vapor. The atmosphere features dense clouds of sulfuric acid.

Venus's surface appears extremely hot and dry. There is no liquid water, because the heat would cause it to boil away. Most of what is known about Venus's surface comes from radar measurements taken by spacecraft. These measurements show that the surface of Venus includes different landforms. About two-thirds of the surface consists of flat, smooth plains. These plains are dotted with thousands of volcanoes. The rest of the planet is marked by mountains, canyons, and valleys.

Like many solid bodies in the solar system, Venus's surface is also marked by **impact craters.** Impact craters are bowl-shaped areas left when a solid object, such as a meteoroid, strikes the ground. Solid surfaces accumulate impact craters over time. But Venus has many fewer craters when compared to the moon and the planets Mars and Mercury. This probably means that the surface of Venus is relatively young—only about 1 billion years old. Also, the planet has probably been resurfaced by volcanic activity, erasing older craters. Such activity may continue today.

9

Inventor feature:
Rocket Man

When Geoffrey Landis was young, his interest in science and space exploration was fed by his involvement in model rocketry.

" In high school, I started designing and building model rockets. Model rocketry was basically my obsession. I spent more time working on rockets than I spent on my schoolwork. **"** —Geoffrey

Model rockets fly the same way as space rockets. But models weigh less than 3 ½ pounds (1.5 kilograms), and they usually measure only 8 to 24 inches (20 to 61 centimeters) long.

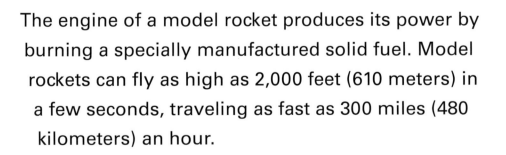

The engine of a model rocket produces its power by burning a specially manufactured solid fuel. Model rockets can fly as high as 2,000 feet (610 meters) in a few seconds, traveling as fast as 300 miles (480 kilometers) an hour.

Large numbers of young people and adults fly model

rockets as a hobby. Most rocketeers build their first rockets with kits sold by hobby stores.

█ At my school, we had a model rocket club. The people I worked with in that club were among my greatest sources of inspiration as a young person. █ —Geoffrey

Local model rocket clubs may be formed around almost any organization, such as a school or youth group. Such clubs may have their own launch systems and other equipment. Many clubs hold model rocketry contests for their members.

Landis setting up a rocket glider.

Several countries have national model rocket organizations. They set up safety rules, certify that model rocket engines meet established standards, issue publications, and approve local clubs. The national organization in the United States is the National Association of Rocketry (NAR) in Marion, Iowa.

Much more information can be found at http://www.nar.org /model-rocket-info/.

Hostile conditions

Venus has some of the worst weather in the solar system. It is far hotter than Earth. It has a dense, crushing atmosphere. And damaging acid rains down onto the surface. These conditions make it extremely difficult to study with **landers.**

Venus has an incredibly thick atmosphere. Atmospheres are made up of gases. Consider Earth's atmosphere—the air. Air is fairly light, and it is always around us. As a result, we do not often think of air as having weight, but it does. The weight of all that gas exerts a pressure on every object on Earth's surface, called **surface pressure.** The surface pressure on Venus is about 90 times that on Earth.

> **"** The surface of Venus is the most hostile environment in the solar system. It has a high-pressure, *corrosive* [destructive] atmosphere and an extremely high surface temperature. **"** —Geoffrey

> **"** That is greater than the pressure ½ mile [0.8 kilometers or 2,640 feet] underwater on Earth. **"** —Geoffrey

For comparison, human divers have trouble surviving the pressure more than 100 feet (30 meters or 0.019 miles) underwater without protection. But all that pressure is nothing compared to Venus's temperature.

Venus's surface can get as hot as about 870 °F (465 °C), hotter than the surface of any other planet. By contrast, the highest temperature ever recorded on Earth was 134.1 °F (56.7 °C) in Death Valley, a desert in the southwestern United States. The temperature on Venus is hot enough to melt lead.

Why is Venus so hot? Mercury is the planet nearest the sun. Yet the surface of Venus is hotter than the surface of Mercury. Most scientists think Venus's extraordinary heat is created by a **greenhouse effect.** An ordinary greenhouse stays warm by letting in sunlight but preventing much heat from escaping. The thick clouds and dense atmosphere of Venus work in much the same way. The energy from sunlight is able to filter down to the planet's surface. But the carbon dioxide and droplets of sulfuric acid prevent much of the solar energy from escaping.

Venus passes in front of the sun in this composite image taken by a spacecraft.

" The temperature at the surface is way hotter than the inside of a household oven. **"** —Geoffrey

Previous
explorations

The only space **probes** ever to land safely on the Venusian surface were part of the **Soviet Union's** Venera program. *Venera* is the name for *Venus* in the Russian language.

The Venera program included dozens of probes sent to Venus during the 1960's, 1970's, and 1980's. Some of these probes just flew by Venus, but others orbited it. Several of the Venera missions included **landers.**

The Venera 7 lander made the first landing on Venus in 1970. In the extreme heat and pressure, the probe lasted only 23 minutes after touchdown. The Venera 9 lander, in 1975, sent back the first image of the planet's surface.

> **❚❚** The extreme heat, **surface pressure,** and sulfuric acid combine to make the surface of Venus tremendously difficult to explore. **❚❚** —Geoffrey

Venera 7 lands on Venus in this illustration. A later probe, Venera 9, took the first picture of the planet's surface (inset).

ВЕНЕРА-9 22.10.1975   ОБРАБОТКА ИППИ АН СССР 28.2.1976

By far the most successful **lander** of the program
was Venera 13, which landed on Venus in 1982.
The **probe** touched down on a broad plain in
Venus's southern *hemisphere* (half). Venera 13 sent
back the first color photographs of the planet's
surface. The fascinating images were mostly of the
ground near the landing site. But they showed a
flat plain marked by broken shapes that may have
been slabs of rock or crusts made of fine particles.
A twin craft, Venera 14, landed two days later.

Venera 13 was designed to last only 30 minutes
after landing. But the craft continued to work on
the surface for 2 hours and 7 minutes. It took a
total of 14 color photographs and 8 black-and-white
photographs. It also drilled into the landing site soil
and found a texture like that of *compacted* (pressed
together) ash on Earth.

Could there be life on Venus? The types of living
things found on Earth could not live on the surface
of Venus, mostly because of the extreme heat.
On Earth, however, certain types of *microbes* (very
tiny living things) have been found living in the
clouds. Though it is unlikely, some astronomers think
that similar microbes could survive in the Venusian
cloud tops, where the temperature is a much milder
55 °F (13 °C).

Engineers from
the Soviet Union
assemble Venera
13, which went on
to take the first
color photographs
of Venus's surface
(below).

19

Inventor feature:
Veteran of Mars

Before Geoffrey Landis turned his attention to Venus, he worked on two landmark **rover** missions sent to explore the surface of Mars.

❝ When I came to NASA, I was put to work designing **solar cells** to power space missions. That was the way I got involved, by working on the power systems. I started by working on anything that needed power. Then I moved into working on power systems that would work on Mars, which got me involved in the Pathfinder mission. ❞ —Geoffrey

Mars Pathfinder was a United States mission that gathered images and other data from the surface of Mars for nearly three months in 1997. After landing, Pathfinder released the Mars Sojourner Rover, a small, six-wheeled robot that analyzed the rocks and soil on Mars. The Pathfinder mission returned more than 16,500 images to scientists on Earth, including spectacular color pictures of Mars's surface and views of the planet's moons and the sun from Mars.

Landis went on to work on the two U.S. Mars Exploration Rovers, which landed on the planet in 2004. The golf cart-sized rovers were designed to operate for 90 days. One rover, nicknamed Spirit, continued to explore the planet for five years. The other, Opportunity, has lasted even longer. By 2016, Opportunity had covered more than 26 miles (43 kilometers)—a Martian marathon.

Spirit and Opportunity sent back detailed images of the planet's ground features. They provided the first good evidence that liquid water once covered large areas of the planet's surface. Together with data from other craft, these missions helped give scientists a fairly detailed picture of Mars's history.

Geoffrey poses with a model of the Opportunity rover.

Roving Venus

Venera 13's haul of 22 photographs and other data was impressive, considering the technology available at the time and the hostile surface conditions on Venus. But this collection is small compared to the vast amount of information gathered by the Martian **rover** missions.

Scientists are looking for ways to learn much more about Venus and its history. For example, scientists think Venus may once have been more like Earth. Several billion years ago, Venus may have had an ocean. The planet may also once have had a climate more like that of Earth. Did Venus once have more water than it does now? And if so, where did the water go? To answer these kinds of questions, scientists will need to learn more about the planet's surface.

" We have been learning a lot about the planet Mars through the Mars rovers. Spirit and Opportunity have been driving around on Mars and teaching us a lot about the planet. The Mars rovers were so efficient at teaching us about Mars. We want to do the same thing with Venus. **"** —Geoffrey

Taking the heat

The best way to learn about Venus may be to send a robotic geologist—a **rover**—to explore the Venusian surface. (A geologist is a scientist who studies rocks, soil, mountains, volcanoes, and other landforms.) But if a rover is to revolutionize our understanding of Venus, it will have to survive the terrible surface conditions for more than a few hours.

What will be the biggest challenge for scientists? The destructive, or corrosive, atmosphere will be a challenge, but it is not the

❚❚ Remember that the pressure at the surface of Venus is the same as that ½ mile [0.8 kilometer] beneath the surface of the ocean on Earth. That might not be comfortable for humans, but submarines regularly operate at that depth. ❚❚ —Geoffrey

biggest problem. Engineers have plenty of practice designing corrosion-resistant materials. The extreme **surface pressure** is not a deal-breaker, either. Engineers know how to seal and shield a rover against such pressures.

The main obstacle to exploring Venus will be the heat.

Engineers know how to build metal rover parts capable of withstanding the searing Venusian heat, but they will also have to figure out how to protect the craft's sensitive **electronics.**

" Nobody has ever tried to build the kind of rover we are talking about that operates at these very high temperatures. That is probably the greatest challenge. " —Geoffrey

Big idea:
High-temperature electronics

Electronics are the computerized, electric-powered devices that help the spacecraft do its work. They include the sensors that the craft uses to take measurements and the control systems that help to guide the craft's operations. Electronics also power the communication systems used to send data gathered by the craft back to scientists on Earth.

A problem with electronics is that they tend not to handle heat well. Modern electronics often rely on **integrated circuits.** Integrated circuits are chips of semiconductor material, usually silicon, etched (carved) with microscopic pathways called circuits. The circuits work by carrying and sorting tiny bits of electricity called electrons.

As an integrated circuit heats up, the resistance of the silicon increases, making it harder for electrons to flow. The more the silicon increases resistance the less likely the integrated circuit will work properly. It might even fail completely, because extreme heat can damage the chip itself.

" Silicon simply does not work when it overheats. "
—Geoffrey

On Earth, the overheating problem is handled through the use of cooling systems. Cooling systems are devices that work to remove excess heat, helping to keep electronics cool. But cooling systems can be heavy and use lots of power. These problems make cooling systems a bad fit for space missions because weight must be kept down and there isn't a lot of available power. Cooling systems can also fail, perhaps leading to the loss of the craft. But, scientists are already working on a solution to this problem.

Big idea:
High-temperature electronics cont.

Rather than rely on cooling systems, engineers at the John Glenn Research Center are working to develop **integrated circuits** that can continue to operate at high temperatures. These chips are designed to function under the increased resistance without failing. They are also made of semiconductor materials that resist heat better than pure silicon, such as silicon carbide.

❚❚ At the NASA Glenn Research Center, we now have a *chamber* [an enclosed space] called the Glenn Extreme Environments Rig [GEER] where we can make surface conditions like those on Venus. GEER has the high pressure, the high temperature, and the **carbon dioxide** atmosphere. We can test the **electronics** under these conditions. **❚❚** — Geoffrey

By 2016, engineers had managed to produce chips that function at up to 660 °F (350 °C). They hope to be able to push that temperature even higher. As with many things in engineering, the solution isn't perfect.

Down to Earth:

An engineer works with the Glenn Extreme Environments Rig, which can replicate (copy) the surface conditions of Venus.

Ideas from space that could serve us on our planet.

One of the reasons people fund space research is that it can have everyday benefits here on Earth. The same high-temperature electronics being studied in the Venus **rover** project are being developed for applications in aviation.

❝ The best high-temperature electronics we can make are about as sophisticated as the silicon electronics of the 1960's. But remember, we were able to make electronics good enough to send astronauts to the moon even with 1960's technology! ❞

—Geoffrey

❝ One of the projects we do at NASA Glenn is to make sensors that can operate inside the hot conditions in a jet engine, so we can find out what is happening inside the engine as it operates. ❞ —Geoffrey

Inventor feature: Science fiction author

❚❚ In addition to being a scientist and an engineer, I write science fiction. ❚❚ —Geoffrey

Landis is an accomplished science fiction author. Some 100 of his short stories have been published, and he has won the Hugo Award and the Nebula Award, two of the most prestigious awards for science fiction.

❚❚ I like writing science fiction because it gives me the ability to let my imagination run wild. I can go as far out into the future and into the solar system as my imagination is willing to go. ❚❚ —Geoffrey

Landis is particularly proud of his novel, *Mars Crossing* (2001). The book tells the story of a third crewed (operated by people) expedition to Mars, following the failures of two previous missions.

Geoffrey Landis (bottom right) at a book signing with fellow science fiction writer Allen Steele.

Cloudy skies ahead

High-temperature **electronics** are only one piece of the puzzle. To move around on the Venusian surface, Landis's **rover** will need a source of power.

❚❚ You cannot have a car without an engine, and you cannot have a rover without a power source to move the wheels. ❚❚ —Geoffrey

Moving the craft around requires much more energy than powering the electronics. The Mars rovers get their power from the greatest power source in the solar system—the sun. The craft use devices called **solar cells** to convert the energy of sunlight into electricity. Engineers love using solar power for space missions, because solar power is often plentiful and does not require heavy, dangerous, or expensive fuels.

❚❚ But it is so hot on Venus that solar cells basically just overheat. It is not that they do not work at all, but that they do not work very well. ❚❚ —Geoffrey

Venus's thick clouds, as seen in this photograph, make it difficult for would-be landers to use solar power on its surface.

❚❚ It is cloudy all the time on Venus. ❚❚ —Geoffrey

Solar cells are essentially **electronic** equipment, and we have learned that such equipment does not function well in the Venusian heat. Also, remember that thick wrapping of clouds.

Only about 1 percent of sunlight makes it through the clouds to the planet's surface. In addition, the clouds seem to be particularly good at blocking blue light, which is the most energetic. The lack of solar energy led Landis to consider a different power source.

❚❚ I asked the question, 'Well, what resources do we have on the planet Venus?' It does have a thick atmosphere. Could we use that atmosphere to propel the rover? Well, possibly we can. Maybe we can drive the rover over the surface of Venus powered by a sail. ❚❚ —Geoffrey

Big idea:
Land sailing

" On Earth, people have made little vehicles that have been driven by the wind. People actually use these for sport. They have races of wind-powered carts in the desert. Nobody has ever tried this on another planet. **"** —Geoffrey

When we think of sailing, we usually think of boats. But people have used sail power to get around on land, too. Sail-powered wagons are described in writings from ancient China. More recently, in the mid-1800's, settlers in the American West experimented with "wind wagons," harnessing the plentiful winds of the American prairie to travel the frontier.

Today, **land sailing** is mainly a form of recreation. Modern land sailors drive around in small, wheeled carts called *sail wagons* or *land yachts*. The first modern land-sailing races were held in the early 1900's.

The sails on today's sailcraft are not just sheets of fabric that catch the wind. Instead, they take on a special shape, somewhat like the wings of an airplane. As air flows over an airplane's wing, the wing's shape helps to produce an upward force called *lift*. Lift is what allows the plane to fly.

In this photograph from the 1910's, a couple poses in an early recreational sail wagon.

In the same way, as the wind blows across a modern sail, the sail's shape helps to produce a force that pushes the craft forward. As the air blows over the sail, this force pushes the sailcraft faster and faster. In this way, sailcraft can actually sail faster than the wind. In 2009, for example, the British land sailor Richard Jenkins set a land-yachting record. In winds of 30 to 50 miles (50 to 80 kilometers) per hour, Jenkins reached a top speed of 121.6 miles (202.9 kilometers) per hour.

Land sailing requires lots of wind and flat, clear ground. As a result, land-sailing races are often held at airfields, on beaches, and on flat, hard deserts.

Getting around

Land sailing involves two main requirements. First, it requires relatively flat, smooth ground.

The second thing land sailing requires is wind. Wind speeds in Venus's atmosphere reach a terrifying 230 miles (370 kilometers) per hour. But close to the surface, they only reach about 6 miles (10 kilometers) per hour. That speed is actually a bit slow for land sailing.

❝ But remember, the air is much thicker on Venus. **❞**
— Geoffrey

Think about the air on Mars. Mars's atmosphere is only about $\frac{1}{100}$ as thick as Earth's. Scientists have observed wind gusts as high as 55 miles (90 kilometers) per hour on Mars. But because the air is so thin, such winds do not have much force.

On Venus, the thicker air can provide more force, or push, even at low speeds. Wind speeds of 2 miles (3 kilometers) per hour should be enough to move a 400-pound (180-kilogram) **rover** over 100 yards in a day.

> The pictures taken by the Venera **probes** show flat, even terrain stretching to the horizon. Such terrain is ideal for land sailing. "

—Geoffrey

In addition to wind, land sailing requires flat ground, as seen in this land-sailing race acoss a beach.

Could land-sailing rovers be useful elsewhere? Venus is not the only destination in the solar system that has wind. Mars has wind, for example, though the air there is probably too thin to make **land sailing** practical.

❚❚ We also have looked at Saturn's moon Titan. Titan is the only moon in the solar system that has an atmosphere. It has a very thick atmosphere, not as thick as that of Venus but about 2 ½ times thicker than Earth's. We have begun to think about looking at Titan to see whether we could operate a sail-powered rover there. ❚❚ —Geoffrey

Saturn's moon Titan is one of the largest moons in the solar system and could be a target for future land-sailing missions.

Inventor feature:
Other Interests

Scientists and engineers do not spend all of their time in labs. They have interests and hobbies just like the rest of us. Geoffrey Landis recently took up the sport of fencing. Fencers compete in sword-fighting competitions using blunted weapons and protective equipment.

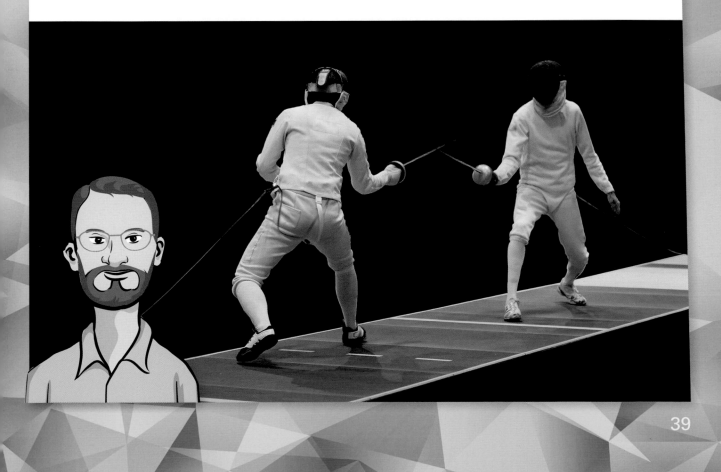

Surfing the Venusian winds

So what might a **land-sailing** Venus mission look like? The mission might include both an **orbiter** and a land-sailing **rover.** Launched from Earth, it might take about five months for the paired craft to get into position. Then the two units would separate. The orbiter would go into orbit around Venus. The rover, packed into a protective covering called an aeroshell, would fall into the planet's atmosphere.

❚❚ There are parts of Venus you can just drive around on with no problem at all. It is a beautiful hard flat surface, like a giant parking lot. At least to start with, we would target someplace that looks pretty easy to drive on. ❚❚ —Geoffrey

Because Venus has a thick atmosphere, parachutes should be sufficient to lower the landing craft to the ground safely. Once the craft has safely landed, the land-sailing rover could come out of its packing and unfold its antenna.

The antenna would enable the rover to communicate with the **orbiter,** which could relay signals to and from Earth. The first pictures sent back would help controllers on Earth determine likely

An artist's initial concept of a land-sailing Venus rover.

❚❚ We will be sailing on Venus. How cool is that? ❚❚ —Geoffrey

targets for exploration. The controllers could then transmit commands for the craft to put up its sail.

Rather than a cloth sail, Landis has designed the craft with a rigid device called an airfoil. The 26-foot- (8-meter-) tall airfoil is somewhat like the wing of an airplane, tilted vertically.

The airfoil surface would be covered in **solar cells,** which even on Venus may supply just enough energy to power the **electronics.** The craft's instruments might include a camera, a drill, and a device called an X-ray spectrometer, used to determine the chemical makeup of rocks.

Landis hopes such a craft, well built and equipped with high-temperature electronics, might continue to operate on the surface of Venus for about 50 days.

❚❚ We will also have shown that we can explore a whole new type of place—a place that is extremely hot. We will be saying that high temperature is no longer a barrier to space exploration. **❚❚** —Geoffrey

The images and other data the craft gathers in that time might well revolutionize our understanding of Venus. The mission could help us understand the forces that shape Venus's surface, keeping it relatively young. It may also give us clues to what Venus was like in the past.

Why study Venus? Venus is an important target of exploration because it is similar to Earth, but with a much different history. The same **greenhouse effect** that warms Venus also warms Earth. The effect plays a major role in *global warming*, an increase in Earth's average surface temperature. So studying Venus could help us understand the forces that shape Earth's climate.

❚❚ Venus is what Earth might be like if it had gone bad early in its history and turned very, very hot. It is useful to learn about how things could have been different. ❚❚ —Geoffrey

Geoffrey Landis and his team

Geoffrey Landis (bottom row, third from right) and the COMPASS (Collaborative Modeling for Parametric Assessment of Space Systems) team.

Glossary

carbon dioxide (KAHR buhn dy OK syd) an odorless, colorless gas that makes up much of Venus's atmosphere.

electronics (ih LEHK TRON ihks) devices, such as computer chips, that work by directing the flow of electricity through them.

greenhouse effect (GREEN hows uh FEHKT) the effect in which gases in a planet's atmosphere allow energy from the sun in but prevent heat from escaping, warming the planet.

impact crater (IHM pakt KRAY tuhr) a bowl-like depression, or dent, left behind by the impact of a solid object, such as a meteoroid.

integrated circuit (IHN tuh GRAY tihd SUR kiht) a chip of semiconductor material, such as silicon, etched with microscopic circuits; a computer chip.

land sailing (land SAY lihng) harnessing the power of the wind to move a land vehicle, such as a cart.

lander (LAN duhr) a spacecraft meant to land on the surface of its target.

orbiter (AWR biht uhr) a spacecraft meant to orbit (move around) its target.

probe (prohb) a robotic spacecraft sent to explore an astronomical target.

rover (ROH vuhr) a spacecraft meant to roll around on the surface of its target.

solar cells (SOH luhr sehlz) electronic devices that turn sunlight into electricity.

Soviet Union (SOH vee eht YOON yuhn) (Union of Soviet Socialist Republics, U.S.S.R.) the world's first and most powerful Communist country. It existed from 1922 to 1991.

surface pressure (SUR fihs PREHSH uhr) the pressure on a planet's surface caused by the weight of the overlying atmosphere.

For further information

Want to know more about Venus?

Simon, Seymour. *Venus.* Starwalk Kids Media, 2012.

Want to know more about sailing?

Davidson, Tim and Steve Kibble. *Sailing for Kids.* Fernhurst Books, Inc., 2015.

Want to know more about atmosphere?

Kjelle, Marylou Morano. *A Project Guide to Wind, Weather, and the Atmosphere.* Earth Science Projects for Kids. Mitchell Lane Publishers, 2010.

Think like an inventor

Land yachts are not the only things that make use of the air to move. Birds, airplanes, and balloons all move with the help of the air. Choose an object or animal (or come up with your own) and research how it uses air to move. Then, use what you learned about movement through air to draw your own Venus **probe.** Be sure you include labels to show the parts of your probe and how it works.

Index

Acknowledgments

Cover	WORLD BOOK illustration by Francis Lea (NASA/JPL/NSSDCA; John D. Sirlin/Shutterstock)
4-5	Neal Simpson (licensed under CC BY-ND 2.0)
6-7	© travenian/Getty Images
8-9	NASA
11	Geoffrey Landis
12-13	© Stocktrek Images/Getty Images
14-15	Solar Dynamics Observatory/NASA
16-17	Buzz Aldrin's Space Program Manager (SPM)/Slitherine Ltd/Polar Motion; NASA/NSSDC
18-19	© Sovfoto/UIG/Getty Images; NASA/NSSDCA/Russian Space Agency
21	NASA
22-23	NASA/JPL-Caltech/MSSS
24-25	NASA/Goddard Space Flight Center Conceptual Image Lab
27	© Poylov Vladimir, Shutterstock
29	GEER/NASA Glenn Research Center
31	© Starship Century
32-33	NASA/Mariner 10/Calvin J. Hamilton
35	Library of Congress
37	© Andia/UIG/Getty Images
38	NASA/JPL-Caltech/Space Science Institute
39	© sezer66/Shutterstock
41	NASA
42-43	WORLD BOOK illustration by Francis Lea (NASA/JPL/NSSDCA; John D. Sirlin/Shutterstock)
44	Geoffrey Landis